# BOOKS BY MARVIN BELL

# RESIDUE OF SONG

# RESIDUE

New York   ATHENEUM

1974

# OF SONG

Poems by

## MARVIN BELL

Acknowledgments are due the following books and periodicals, in whose pages some of these poems previously appeared: THE AMERICAN POETRY REVIEW, CHICAGO TRIBUNE MAGAZINE, CONCERNING POETRY, FIELD, THE GODDARD JOURNAL, HEARTLAND II (Northern Illinois University), JEWISH-AMERICAN LITERATURE (New American Library), THE MAJOR YOUNG POETS (World), NEW AMERICAN REVIEW, POETRY, STAND, and WOO HAVOC (Barn Dream).

The following poems appeared originally in POETRY: *Death of a Critic, The Present, Temper, To the Sky,* and *Travels We Took in Our Time.*

*Impotence* appeared previously as a broadside published by The Valley Press in 1972. *Anthropological* appeared previously as a broadside published by The Slow Loris Press in 1971.

The following poems are reprinted from WOO HAVOC, published in a limited edition by The Barn Dream Press in 1971: *Impotence, Set in Hollywood Hills, Anthropological, What You Are, Temper, Song of the Immediacy of Death, The Home Front, Little Father Poem, Gratitude,* and *The Present.*

The epigraph to section III is a Yiddish proverb.

LIBRARY OF CONGRESS CATALOG CARD NUMBER 74-80325
ISBN 0-689-10637-8
PUBLISHED SIMULTANEOUSLY IN CANADA BY MC CLELLAND AND STEWART LTD.
COMPOSITION BY H. WOLFF, NEW YORK
PRINTED AND BOUND BY THE MURRAY PRINTING COMPANY,
FORGE VILLAGE, MASSACHUSETTS
DESIGNED BY KATHLEEN CAREY
FIRST EDITION

*To my sister, Ruby*

# CONTENTS

## III *Being in Love*

## IV *Holding Together*

## V *Song of the Immediacy of Death*

*If you can't get up, get down;*
*if you can't get across, get across.*
YIDDISH PROVERB

# I

# Study of the Letter A

# HERE

on Venus, time passes slowly because
we are all preoccupied with love.
The trees build up like sponges,
the crust under us accumulates like coral,
we begin to feel the long pressure
the jewel feels, if the jewel feels,
and, although this is suspicious belief,
we welcome the illusion with that thrill
formerly reserved for the profane.
His hands are under her buttocks;
her legs are bent on his shoulders;
their extensions are the piping for
"the best that has been thought or said."
The image is of a brain for all space.
The universe, remember, is a ribbon
where we follow back to the beginning
and so meet that one of whom you were thinking
when you mistook being here for being there.

# RESIDUE OF SONG

You were writing a long poem, yes,
about marriage, called "On Loneliness."
Then you decided not to.
There was a certain inconsolable *person*.
You felt you had to discover who.
You would be shocked to discover it was
not yourself. Yourself!, yourself!,
as if the whole world were but glass
for your splendid insights, put softly.
Who was it walked the length of the lawn,
crossed over into a brilliance you knew came
from another world, but from where?
She was out walking, and you were afraid for the
children!
Had she taken out a knife? Had she
pledged her return though nothing changed?
Had she even realized how *wilful* all this was:
hysteria, dry heaving, the throat crawling
with sounds ground down from expectation,
because you lied to her about—was it
other women? No. Because you told the truth,
of course that was a kind of weeping
as if unto Mother, for approval and pointers.
Yes, yes, you expected understanding
and refreshed company, since you were the lonely.
It was as if you had been waiting on the corner,
with who knows what exploits  seemingly on your
lapels,
when *she* walked by: not forked prey, but a friend!
You brought her your past; she wept.
She brought you her future; you mislaid it,

*4*

later you squeezed until it uttered, *piano,*
"Where are we? Where, for that matter, were we
when we met? I was out walking, and you,
coming from shadow, postured like the children
we agreed upon. Amidst wickedness, we were the age,
if the age was wicked, but safe on the surface.
Suddenly, we were responsible for discourse, whereas,
years earlier, we had been held only by the moon.
What did you tell the others then, over your shoulder,
calling me to stop you—that you would never?
One appointment leads to another in these soft days.
A photograph of flowers the skin remembers,
a bowl of leaves before the kitchen screen,
is to this life as you are to mine. Your cries,
for ecstatic madness, are not sadder than some things.
From the residue of song, I have barely said my love
again,
as if for the last time, believing that you will leave me."

# ANTHROPOLOGICAL

It is too easy to say
a stone grows inside the man,

too easy to say
the pit flowers in his genitals.

It is too easy to say
his bones are growing outwards

like the points of stars,
too simple

to say he ripens
in the smell of the horses,

the beaks of the birds,
the long bodies of the feathers

and leaves. You are too clever
under the boulders,

deep in the tar-pits,
digging for armor.

No more fossils
of eunuchs!

# STUDY OF THE LETTER A

A fine A reaches from the soft center
of the skull of a man to either side
of his chin and crosses his face at
the eyes, just as the bridge of the nose
runs the eye of the listener
from eyes to mouth and back again.
The speaker's face itself describes
a square from chin to hair and ear to ear.

The page on which the A appears
in turn's a magic square, undescribed,
neither Satanic nor Diabolic,
like chess in Moscow. Or like ancient
Wisdom, seated squarely on square stone,
while Fortune from a round seat was pleased
this way or that way but never one way.
Some people we will come to are like this.

For now consider the structure of
the fossil sponge: like monkey bars.
Or certain Hittite characters, or semaphores.
The square, pure form of complete idea,
wards off plagues and catches our colds.
We will not see many people in the square.
No deity and no human being lives in this place,
except one woman chosen by the god.

# PORTRAIT IN CHURCH

*Life consists of propositions about life.*
STEVENS

You "sit" in church, as for a portrait.
Enormous sorrow.

Your face is deeply cut
but closes.

Your face is lovely, closes,
when I try to see beyond.

Elsewhere, the astronaut cranes
to see Earth where he first saw Heaven.

Elsewhere, children killed in war
are somehow perfect, seen to be perfect

as slaughter is the form of mankind's
form so far, whoopier under bomby skies.

Did I forget what's closest to my heart?
Ache, peril, fissure, clot and blast.

A man may be easily confused,
one for the other notwithstanding.

And the maniac's me. The manic's panic's
mine. It's been that or a headstone.

The life is seamless; the livelihood, not.
I went lie-detecting among the young poets.

The aspirations of those *ingenues*
lilt and flutter in a choir of make-work.

Finally, I was unable to decide
whether I wanted to know the truth

or be loved. With you in church,
I am held by the stained glass,

by the angelic child in the foyer who
is dusted all the way to his face each day.

Translucence and that stone child:
appearances turned pretty, to cause.

It doesn't matter
that the grown-up is in pain, the child dead,

elsewhere, elsewhere. In here,
we are little tubes of goodness,

sure faces shining
with the message that must get out.

If it was bad today, tomorrow will be better.
While out there, tomorrow will be worse.

# VIET NAM

is a place you will hear of
"in the future,"
which is not to say tomorrow merely,
over which a great peace
will have fallen, much as
the wool coverlet my love repaired
on my thirty-fifth Christmas
settles on my midday escapes to the couch.
This was a grimy coverlet, but pretty,
from the store of the Salvation Army
where I found too the long photo
of fading doughboys, the first tin soldiers,
and a loud five-buck castoff loveseat.
I hate to admit the uses we make of these:
nostalgia, sexual and so forth.
Another memento is a golden turtle-clock,
and when the alarm under its shell unwinds
some lot of time we marked is ended.
Though we know better about time,
we know nothing about peace,
which is a function of time and war
and which we can get from anything but people.

# THE PRICE IS RIGHT

They turned over the wrong card but then
the right card and the girl won two motorcycles.
She can ride them one at a time or
both together, and her husband if she has one
can go on ahead in the family car.
We've come so far on the wheel we can't
look back for fear of falling, though one man
survived a crash that I know of. Some of you might
remember the plane that fell in Brooklyn,
from which a burning child was the only survivor
but died in shock a day later. If you can't
talk about it without throwing up, there's
some hope for you but no future.

# ARISTOTLE

He put in their places as much as he had time for,
and though the word for this is missing
in its entirety we know he knew how it feels
when the hurt and humiliation defeat
guts and gravity to come up out of us
shouting about art instead of murder and giving
to pain the high-sounding name of "tragedy"—
which is a fall from a high place by a weak
sister; *i.e.*, you can jump from a skyscraper
and learn nothing from doing.

# SHIT

Sometimes I think I could just
get rid of it all, and I know the Yogis
string their noses and rag their stomachs
but that isn't what I mean. It oozes
from braincells the way honey slips from
combs. Finally the life inside leaves too
and some parasite creature takes the candy
and the whole structure, which was once
thick and strong, is like paper. There's
always someone who likes the delicate paper,
like me, because you can imagine it full
of sweetness and labor. Before the combs I
picked up yesterday fall apart completely,
I'd like to get something about them to read
in the bathroom, the place for prose.

# II

# You Would Know

*thirteen poems to my father*

# ORIGIN OF DREAMS

Out from muted bee-sounds and musketry
(the hard works of our ears, dissembling),
under steeply-held birds (in that air
the mind draws of our laid breathing),
out from light dust and the retinal gray,
your face as in your forties appears
as if to be pictured, and will not go away.

I have shut up all my cameras, really,
Father, and thought I did not speak to you,
since you are dead. But you last;
are proved in the distance of a wrist.
Your face in dreams sends a crinkly static
and seems, in its mica- or leaf-like texture,
the nightworks of the viscera.

But feeling's not fancy, fancying you.
I don't forget you, or give stinks for thanks.
I think I think the bed's a balcony,
until we sleep. Then our good intentions
lower us to the dead, where we live.
I think that light's a sheet for the days,
which we lose. Then we go looking.

# IF YOU LIVED IN MOSCOW

We've got the morning—that much
we still have, no thanks to the Tsar.
If you lived in Moscow, you'd appreciate
those black cauldrons they melt the snow in—
the dirty snow only, doing the sun's work.
The Russian white acacia's also American:
our hard black locust, straight to the boatyard!

You had its drugs and gums and cures,
and had cucumber seeds to cool passions!,
but it's that acacia that still interests me.
Is this because a wounded man
cut trees from paper, and made in this way
for himself a sacred wood? I do remember
in your town the kids picked up the corpses.

He, him, his—used by us of the enemy
at all times. Even more so, formerly.
For now the lonely poet resents
any imitation of his and his father's
past happiness, in a boat or on the shore.
Your Russia, without you, is cold and desolate,
of difficult access and of no importance.

# FATHER AND RUSSIA

I see you by thin, flighty apple trees,
picking fruit out of the branched air,
find you in a hand of ice, of which one-third
only appears to welcome but forbid at once.
No, it was only more snow I saw, freezing
completely the fists and fingers of the fruit trees.
You had no intention to smile away your orchard.

Mother Russia's iron militia's a monster,
the thunder of Cossack horses
is a long storm you lip-read the Tsar by.
Your mother knuckles the washboard into your teens,
but plans your escape. Your father sends money.
You in your orchard still fill the wooden baskets,
while the too-long-perfect bruise and fall.

Now I want you as you were before they hurt you,
irreparably as you were as in another country.
The harvest moon, sunset's clockwork, can show us
what to pick, but not whom to pick on.
Step here with me, and stay, and blame the birds
whose unschooled bedlam in the sweltering cherries
is all the blame and harm a tree can bear.

# WHO KILLED CHRIST?

The square is as high and as wide
as a man with his arms outstretched.
The Hebrew letter is blasphemous
to a Christian world. In a Christian world,
the blasphemous Hebrew letter
is the name of God, and the name of God
is like unto the name of the Father,

Father. Every man will be a tree,
may become a shaft stars rain down.
"He-who-labored" came unto me
and I gave him rest: in seeds, pools and poems,
I pardoned the water for no man
can swim in the channel, I let the father
assume all the shapes of the tides,

and I stood against the forsaken beaches
and cried to say something to insult you.
Now the children are scared of the beast-face
at the window, and the window fears cold,
unless I miss my guess, the plants too
have their feelings, the animals don't worship,
so I stand here looking out for no one.

# LETTING IN COLD

Who killed Christ?—my favorite subject.
You misunderstood my love for Russia,
going so far you changed love into hate,
which was not my intention. You know,
in your time you changed life into death,
what-is to what-is-not, schooling to recess.
The enigmatic lesson in geography! that

wasn't the teacher's way of instructing
but only my way of trying propriety.
The proper study of man is where he came from!
You came from Russia—under the hayloads,
bareback to Poland, steerage to America.
The tip of the whip the teacher withdraws
comes all the way from a bitter Europe.

Today, here, the first new snow
bothers the softness in people, and they are kind.
In four months, the world will seem harsh
as ever, a localness, a locking-out that continues,
and we will stand corrected, half-dead and
corrected. No one approaches the father's thoughts
where he stands, at the back door, letting in cold.

## FOLLOWING

Your eye at the glass proves snow
falling now for an unseen hour.
Depth is all. We waited for Christmas.
Two Island ducks would stuff us.
We'd nap it off. Then scavenge the birds.
One done wishbone would not suffice,
nor one wish, granted, fill us.

The rain that rose and fell, rose until
it changed to hail: those stones were large,
injurious, but we thought "marbles."
As in a pantry one thought of spicedrops,
and thought, too, the *kchunk* of the pump
a linking of water to water. One wanted to.
When I was there when you were there,

I wanted to. I also could fancy
that if one thing were like another
your being there was like your not being there,
if I paid attention. It was hard to follow.
Our house was a playhouse. You were my father.
The scattershot of ice, the chain-making of a pump,
were the rising sounds of your falling, better thought-of.

# GARLIC

Russian penicillin—that was the magic
of garlic, a party and cure. Sure,
you'll wrestle the flowers for fixings,
tap roots and saw branch for the ooze
of health, but you'll never get better.
I say you're living a life of leisure,
if life is life and leisure leisure.

The heart's half a prophet; it hurts
with the crabapple floating on top,
it aches just to know of the ocean—
the Old Country split off from the New—
and the acts of scissors inside you.
The heart of the East European,
poor boiler, is always born broken.

The sore heart weighs too much
for its own good. And Jewish health
is like snow in March, sometimes April.
The brothers who took their medicine
with you (garlic!) are dead now too.
The herb that beat back fever and sore
went home to its family: the lilies.

# FROM A DISTANCE

The tree will not ask for relief
though covered by sores and parasites
and misunderstood for a very long time.
Our shelled acorns and scalloped ivy,
our aromatic mint—trodden sentry—
are but underfooting for the wafer-
thin and hollow-needled snow

already bowing toward us under pressure
of a wet summer. An "early Iowa winter scene"
resembles a body, exquisitely blemished,
not lying but reclining as if modeling,
looking neither to the East nor the West,
and strangely! holding in place these shorn trees
we had passed by the mile without thankfulness.

But that is all changed. We lived on "the Island"—
New York's peninsular duck farm—
where the isolate fish-crow in the pine
gave a robber's thanks, and flew like a gash
through the air for the eggs of the others.
We were as far from the cities as I am from you,
which is not so far, Father, as you are from me.

# DEMARCATIONS

The line between water and ice
is strychnine, a kind of nightshade.
The distance between the two of us, Father,
is poison, likewise time turned to substance,
as the first snow turns brief movements
between endless youth and unending age.
This white dust is everywhere!

This white dust everywhere is also
at the hooks of the quarter-moon this evening,
foretelling snow with a pompous emphasis.
Powder tumbles from the punctured capsule,
the peonies tuck and cower from harm,
the book of growth is closed,
and the man in winter bites down hard.

One summer I lived on the edge of, not in,
the Mad River. It was beautiful there, like trout,
and high class. Not like rainbow-less Ralston Creek
running brown past my winter house,
filling up on neighborhood knickknacks.
Elsewhere, I said that night was the distance.
This is the creek that travels that distance.

## THE THUMB AND ONE FINGER MAKE ZERO

O, anything will do
to sink a song to you; I don't ask much.
Here's a glove, a factory "hand,"
encrusted fingers living in mold,
washed and pounded by snow for months,
now reaching from its elastic wrist
for all the world like someone buried.

Wherever's a pebble, there's a grave.
I go to work driving the gravel
that leads the dead here to highway.
Never blinding, it folds back the light
to the underworld, the rich dead.
You took some with you, and left lots more.
(And I was richer when you were poor.)

It's easy to miss you. I start for work,
maybe the roads "turn" into stairs,
the snowflakes placing their flat silence,
the clouds like faces refusing permission.
You see, it's winter. And much is covered.
But loss fits me like the gloves I leave.
I don't know where they turn up, or whether.

# MEMORIAL DAYS

He wears the weather; the grave is soft,
so soft I sink in old warnings:
"Walk on the dead; they'll walk in your head."
—Should I stay away? . . . or whistle.
So soft and drawn, so undergrown,
for now the sucking, heartless plot
could pass for flesh.

Memorials flash; I was the echo,
played second taps better than solo.
A little brave, far gone in the graveyard,
I ached the sweet cornet with sympathy;
then lingered, skipping the march for home.
How many were dead, and all at once?
—A child could wonder, whatever for.

My horn of plenty. I bled their hearts.
The granite markers gave me my measure,
and my directions. First, I shook sugar
out from those stones, waving the echo—
and whistled to stay the way I'd come
by cuts that led the polished stonecutters
to keep the untended, just within earshot.

# TRYING TO CATCH FIRE

You go out when the sky is dark brown,
and the air is thick lotion,
though your son says the sky is still blue
(the son's job is to say it is the same).
You go out when the best drink on earth
is water, and the sun is a lion on fire
still, but gone from your sight and mind.

The son's job is to say the future
(maybe high blue will stand over us tomorrow).
When the sky is dark brown, you go out
and turn your thoughts to the bushes and your face
to the lithe tops of trees, whereas some
are stunted and some are twisted and then some
are old and wrinkled and they are perfect.

You stand close as possible to the perfect ones,
waiting for lightning. While you wait,
you worry an old saw: that the tree is "like"
a family, its branches to high heaven
(and there, blue lustre or age's browning),
its roots sucking life from the dead. That's
a thought you can follow, inside, where you do.

# YOU WOULD KNOW

That you, Father, are "in my mind,"
some will argue, who cherish the present
but flee the past. They haven't my need
to ask, What was I? Asking instead,
What am I?, they see themselves bejewelled
and wingèd. Because they would fly and have value,
their answers are pretty but false:

the fixings of facile alchemists,
preferring their stones to brains.
The brain, remember, is not fool-proof
either, and does and does until it can't.
Sodden, quivering, crossed and recrossed,
the mind can become a headstone
or be malice stuffed with fish.

Everything changes so quickly. You who were
are no longer and what I was I'm not.
Am I to know myself, except as I was?
The rest is catchy, self-promising, false.
O please write to me, and tell me.
I just want to be happy again. That's
what I was, happy, maybe am, you would know.

# III

# Being in Love

*Too bad, the bride is so pretty.*

# IMPOTENCE

Suddenly her breast has never been larger.
All night she's been on your back.
How can you tell her your testicles have fallen off?
It's serious alright. It's just the beginning.
(When the balls go, can the penis be long behind?)
Soon you'll be left with nothing but scar tissue
where once you were the cock of the walk.
Soon you'll be the laughing stock of Niagara Falls.
It's no delight you've got yourself over this barrel.
You knew how far down it was from the beginning.
All those years you were combing it out of your hair,
the hair itself was falling out. If now you're exposed
as the foolish romantic, why that's what you deserve,
Foolish Romantic. You wanted orgasm and repose.
You wanted love without memory. You earnestly desired
beautiful women in bondage, their feelings held hostage,
and for a while there, you were right in the thick of it.
Now you have the lowest membership of all.
Now you are nothing anyone would love.
Now you are a figure of total submission.
So what if you could do anything once.
(Why are you even bringing up these matters of taste?)
Now the end is near. Now you limp along.
Goodbye, A. Goodbye, B. Don't hate me, C. Farewell, D.
I'm not letting you go. Just turning you over for a while.

You said, "My husband . . ." without alarm,
but were frightened. The couch, like soft soap,
welcomed our sinking reserves for a last tumble.
Were we so evil? Was he in such a hurry?
Was there anything, given time, I'd steal?

Who could not love this little boy's fantasy?—
the sun breaking its applause on the jalousies,
my heart in your apartment with many legs,
a pulse alien to nostalgia because racing,
and then—the intimate form of "you" which is

"I remember." Your spiky umbrella plant
fingered us with shadow to which we could look
up as if luxurious under Southern palms,
but we were in the North just before winter,
don't forget that we grew cold to one another.

Why now use your absence to write of love?
To recoup a lost experience? Or something deeper?
"At the right time" seems to suggest
a moment of crisis, while "nothing else ever was"
implies that nothing but a pair of lovers . . .

Do you still resemble my chance at youth?,
or the bouncy plastic clowns kids box:
expressions of living falsity—like mummies.
Whatever you meant to me, the palm is smooth again,
giving airs to the past: the inflation, the blow-up.

Can the "long years before" be unburied by my poem?
(1)Who knows if hard knocks are fool's gold?
—A mineral is hard; we are only relentless.
Or: (2)I wanted a woman who knew exhaustion
but you were never to be finished, merely abandoned.

## LOVE POEM

Unable to distinguish, O plastic dispensation
for which I longed—modeling oneself this way
then that way, unable to distinguish, unwilling

but always your ass, this carbon telephone
if I pick it up as in a salute
if I pick it up and pick it up and pick it up

I salute the black patch, the euphemistic area,
the little wiry nest we call home O
I am spending my wrist for a triangle

not that these abstractions do not intrigue me:
the double lean-to, the 10 we have made and made
together, the number of the times we wanted

to be sentimental, vulnerable, pesty to desire
and I wanted to be you, demanding nothing
everything would be a substitute for not having you

take me

# BEING IN LOVE

with someone who is not in love with
you, you understand my predicament.
Being in love with you, who are not
in love with me, you understand my dilemma.
Being in love with your being in love
with me, which you are not, you understand

the difficulty. Being in love with your
being, you can well imagine how hard it is.
Being in love with your being you,
no matter you are not your being being in
love with me, you can appreciate and pity
being in love with you. Being in love

with someone who is not in love, you know
all about being in love when being in love
is being in love with someone who is not
in love being with you, which is
being in love, which you know only too well,
Love, being in love with being in love.

# SET IN HOLLYWOOD HILLS

You are such lively lovely animals
as inhabit the inaccessible
tan cliffs though nothing grows there.
You are those strong signals
my whole head is a beam for receiving
from the beaches where my desire
was wet more than we remember.
Guess what? —We get to drink again tonight
in our separate refrigerated bedrooms.

I love you. I don't even know you.

The face of the clock makes time
more De Luxe than we knew it in childhood.
I am growing up because I can't have you.
And no one touches, or touches by
speaking, in your sunny city.
Everyone is so busy. And successful.
The beach is only a paperweight
to hold down the executive's elusive script
of those illusory lives you star in.

My life, my love: I don't even know you.

I want you to give up being a dictionary.
I want you to stop your familiar quotations.
I know a *hundred* Shakespeares.
I know many Mozarts, Hitlers too,
Napoleons and Josephines, Juliets to Romeos.
I want you to be life after death, deceasing.
I want you to have a heart attack, figuratively,

over me, a final inability at work.
I want you to love me, and let me explain:

poorly, undramatically, not without touching.

## WHAT YOU ARE

High on the road, returning from no sleep,
you kept time to the windshield's wipers
by wiping away the stories of hard times:
the heavy heart of the heroine of your marriage
(now broken) deftly blown up and let sail;
the jugular vein of her incomplete suicide
let fall like a slice of your own vain life.

And O you thought it fitting in bad weather
to be out in the cold, without pity or purse
to dry you, who loved to personify tragedy
as your best friend, seeking you everywhere.
You ought to know, this is one more example
that the story (or poem) into which light strikes
is of its own making: Look-a-like; Liar!

# DISSOLUTION

Thomas L. dissolves in the Atlantic
and washes up, just before dinner,
where you and I are nibbling each other.

In our passion, we prepared
for flying barn boards, spaghetti lives,
but this—we thought, leaving our families,

reunion, with its thick gravy, would never
follow us, and we were selfish and glad,
until you, T., ruined our appetites.

Walk on water—the soul can be Romantic;
the body's a stone, a burden,
or a joke.

Yesterday they dug up the magician
who promised to stay buried for two days,
and he was dead. He couldn't even cough.

I love those movies wherein the hero
is a fraud, but after his exposure,
there remain certain unaccountable phenomena.

I believe love is unaccountable too,
and persists when the lady leaves you,
sick on the sight of your dead friend.

As the magic part of that buried-alive act
was the promise and not the outcome,
so the love portion of our romantic dinner

was nowhere to be seen,
itself dissolved, itself known only
by the cheap homage we afford

in letters, headstones,
the false life of the lover in our mind
as we start to swim the ocean.

# IV

# Holding Together

# THE FAMILIAR

The irreversible tendril upon tendril
extending without intending to hold together,
but holding together, the life of the tree
is our life together, Love, extending. You
and I are walking under the umbrella these trees
make of the love of light and why not.

[A sweep of the hand, this second, is continuous,
like the carrier of radio interrupted by voices.
We must not pretend we know what's expected of us
though coming into one's own one notices the familiar,
as the land slants upward from back of the house
as far as possible and blocks our view of Switzerland.]

To have come to a head at a dramatic point,
the light hesitated. We think the stars are cheerful,
precious stations, dear dirt like ourselves. But no.
If the stars are jewels, you are mine here.
If markers are needed, a forest will do. And
if night is the distance, we start together.

# A MORNING

It's all over for the 19th Century,
in which I was progressing
to fame, wealth, women and the present.
"You mean pink flowers, not 'weeds.' "
I arrive by a mystical process in the bedroom.

My wife, the proof in the pudding,
and my two sons—proof . . . of?—
attend me; Nathan, Jason and Dorothy:
two gifts of God and a healer.
But I have difficulty leaving my dream.

As the sore light stubbornly ripens,
and things are replaced by the names of things,
I blunder from bed to fiction.
"Long poem" sounds like "walk home."
I was just there; now it's overgrown.

# BEGIN HERE

How is a shirt like death,
before dawn, losing the blackness,
already the spit echoing hoarsely
in the throat, tranquillity before
sledgehammers, up this early before
anyone to pick pants and shirt?

Is this the shirt you will die in?
Then a shirt is like death, and changes
life. Or is this a shirt you will
advance in, a handsome appearance
for a feeling like lugging stones?
The skin, too, is a pressed shirt,

worn by the roads snarling inside.
A blue road wears a blue cover,
or so it seems; as a red road, red.
To lose your shirt is to lose your
life, a gamble the hooded heart takes
because you are buttoned up in front.

## ABOUT THAT

Love sells off a wilderness in which
blindness is a sort of marshy duty
and a weedy wrestle in all seasons.
Through dry eyes, it wasn't France,
but Montreal. The roads wound easily
to *Mont Royal*, the mountain sat ringed
by worn color, and the ringing just rang

and rang (echoes of missed ethics).
One might survive after all, it can
even be said you supped to suffer
on the word "delectable," which she was.
There is the nervousness of parchment,
and a haughty anxiety, while she waits.
There are the quaking leaves in the fall.

Where is she now, your Canadian girlfriend?
Leaf-taking has turned to winter,
the rains to crystal, and that love,
which was once an exhalation of flowers,
deeds you now the hardhack of the plains.
Some of the land is hilly here, and some flat;
and the heart, the same. And that is that.

# POETRY; THE LOVE OF

The love of technical innovation
brings the lover up on his haunches
as if grovelling and praying at once
to enter the kingdom of Eros.
Wanting and fearing, soft and stony,
he rides to deliver the dead weight.

. . . This indecision, these files of regrets,
these two parts into which all manics are divided,
these anchors on the testicles,
these bare limbs beckoning even in the worst poems,
this natural providence, this death in the family,
these choice decisions among women. . . .

Still love, I saw again, was no solution,
into which one dives for impregnation—
its pure coating applied at great cost.
Love, you come back like so many Puritans,
the leisure of a slow burn, and then—
you forbid me even to write to you.

# I WANTED

I wanted the poem to be God,
that's why, like a translucent glass mobile,
it contains several church windows,
and carries, like the shelf at Land's End
where we meet again our beginnings,
an altar of chalk.

The coveted redness, the whip,
the squalid, and worm-eaten, and chary,
were welcome, the rich and the poor
in myself were acceptable so long as
you found it. And when you found it,
what did I think you would do with it?

So the sun rises, a celestial whelp,
and the scarred moon, in its black hollow,
rests while we wrestle.
Our Conscience, who was in Heaven,
be with us here. For torture the Lord's
answer, the sky is still falling.

# THE CHANCE

I am the last "poet-of-the-family"
before the argument loses its teeth
like a child, skins its tender knees
begging your hand, spreads itself out
to your knife and goes its unplanned way
because no one thinks they want it.

The orgasm is chaotic, better, a chance
for a new life in a perfect world.
If these children are not a mirror,
elaborately bordered, unfinished,
in which a coin reappears in the distance,
projections of "would" and "would not,"

semblances of work save we think of them
childishly, if this mirror is not a good one, . . .
O Jason, "healer," littlest son, read on.
If freedom's only the feeling of freedom,
freedom from feeling's not that; listen!
it's your father who loves the sweet nothings.

# FROM IOWA

It's the winter of mind-over-matter,
or you are locked into . . . ,
and a signal comes miles from almost nowhere
sliding on the snow; crusts of
bread look this welcomingly
through the cold wherever placed
so when a bird comes by, as a bird

he is a harbinger. Spring's building.
We're in no hurry. A light shines far,
like a star. A fire burns.
(The fire's finished; the light's done for.)
Between our fire and their's,
in the center's a soft place, like
the center of a baby's skull,

the place which signalled Soft
and Dangerous, sons, when I held you.
Here's love. Here's friendship for what's
over there, and there's it *in kind*.
But to go from here to there, swervingly,
to miss the edges, is hard but what you have to do,
though it's not yet on your minds to send back word.

# V

# Song of the Immediacy of Death

# LITTLE FATHER POEM

We must stay away from our fathers,
who have big ears. We must stay away
from our fathers, who are the snow.
We must avoid the touch of the leaves
who are our proud fathers. We must
watch out for father underfoot. Father
forgave us when we did nothing wrong,
Father made us well when we were healthy,
now Father wants to support us
when we weigh nothing, Father in his grave
gives us everything we ever wanted,
in a boat crossing who-knows-where,
mist flat over the water,
the sand smooth because soft.

# NEVER SAY DIE

*one to E. D.*

It's bad luck.
It's what you've done lately.
The heart can live on loneliness
and never falter. The heart that lives
on loneliness will miss
but does not falter. And you will
not falter, who
break your life across your knee,
who write to others.

This is my letter to your world;
as shadow lives in substance, lives
also go on among shadows and,
later, in so many cells—
o not so unfortunate!—as may
swell to hold the talk of you.
So I talk of you; as others, me.
You stand for many who wish to,
but cannot, be apart.

# TEMPER

The seed, in its grave,
is the firmest line of labor.
A man woos havoc to undertake
the destruction of a dam in a drought.

Weren't you wound up to be metal
rulers for the hocus-pocus?
The great face of the earth
is pained to be nothing without you:

a sopping interdependence
to make bricks from mud and a family
from seed, and anger
clear through to the center.

*Place* became "enough" and "too much"
together, *leaving* became our future.
We had not hoped to be describing
such endless country, nor did we intend
unconscious directions in such weathers.

So we tried saying "here!" and "stop,"
and *did* stop, and stayed, and would settle
if the miles we could think of only
were the miles that returned us to here,
and if *they* were not miles to be covered.

# THE PRESENT

We wrapped up a trip to Mexico
and handed it over, placed
under the tree a day of fishing,
no fish but fresh air, memory
of hiking, the mountains revisited.

Under the snow, detectable,
a movement of flowers hesitated upwards
to be the gift of the future,
once, to conquer by surprise everywhere,
to grow, to blossom, to be overwhelmed.

# TO THE SKY

*in memory of H. R.*

We are green with our haggard deities.
Yet we are each virgin fortress.

We are prayer like a net
beneath the story of fall.

We are stones asking stars.
We will be sweet dust.

# SONG OF THE IMMEDIACY OF DEATH

The beautiful fans of snow,
the exquisite blossoms of white,
the evaporation of the month,

the flakes of sleepy desire,
these miniature explosions,
these ancestral pleasures,

the bodies of the vapor,
your hurt father
falls, why has he chosen

to crumple his parachute,
everyone surrounds him,
they fall slowly, o sure.

# THE HOME FRONT

German submarines were an idea we watched
off the south shore of Long Island;
two newsmen drove and acted suspiciously
all night to prove two spies could;
I spent afternoons at the Bay
watching for unidentified airplanes;
the Lockheed Lightnings were beautiful
with box tails; nights, I was *on the air,*
mobile. Listening to the news,
I kept track on the flap of a carton
of captured and killed: we were way ahead;
we wanted the war to come closer:
we made up stories for the Coast Guard
in which the Germans were monsters.
But we could never be taken prisoner,
not by a long shot, not while the tide
went out under our care.

# DEATH OF A CRITIC

*W.*, *1900–1968*

I look up into the death of my father,
as I have always done, and the landscape
he passes—a few trees, white winter bark,

the cool clean streets ending in fog,
several short coastal steeples, lighthouse,
and that farther knowledge which locates

as objects he must leave: buoy and flag,
channel, inlet and harbor, and the horns
of salvage and unfriendly witness.

How shall we conclude he fell down?
—Poor man, he could not walk on water.
The first day the hungry showed up to wait.

May he be hidden forever from disaffection
but not from my love, nothing ascend
to meet me, though his work overcome his triumph.

# GRATITUDE

We come to this forest like small change.
The hands, in pockets, are happy to be poor!

# INTRODUCTION

Just as this is no time to be bringing up the subject,
today the benefits of the family concern us,
though surely the subject shall suffer in the midst of
                                                    discussion
in its absence. As what proceeds proceeds by opposites,
the subconscious upward-floating as always if left alone
with its squiggly comics-characters
not looking at all like the hot toads of the surrealists,
so it is clear that a study, say, of the eagle
will describe America completely by taking the eye
of the student into the sky anywhere, zingy!
And research into the family, which is just ending,
starts here. For here we are equals in poverty,
unless you have brought along more than appears.
Take your hands from your pockets and wear them
                                                    openly.
All that's required's good posture, by which
we mean a mind that does not slump nor bow beneath
                                                    feet.
Our intention, unfashionable, is to be wise.
One hopes the terrain will not prove familiar,
though the safety devices we have packed and packed
                                                    may
ruin our sincere hopes of finding a new place.
Still, we set out with our hearts, which are good,
and our teachers' warnings uncorrected by experience.
Wish us well. For now we are in danger, from ourselves.

## ON THE WORD "POSTURE" IN THE
## PRECEDING

Art is to life, today, as beauty/history is to fact.
We may invoke the authority of either.
Sufficiency of argument is lovely ours in either case!
The word "posture" in the foregoing
derives from history as biography does not. In "plain"
truth, no one ever lived as supposed.
The biography, a posture, approximates a man
with ticklish ribs, a shrew for a witch doctor
and a deep-seated need to bully the sublime, whooey.
Phew! Tired of the place and people, where's to go?
Thus, it is preferable to be far-and-away "not tired of."
No fatigue, in fact, will afflict us if we adopt
posture, and give up on our biographies. Still,
we may often be tired in art, faint wisdom,
in works made from weakness, neurosis and crisis—
as if an island could be made from the just-departed
                                                  sands!
Oh no. Here comes the dredger where I lived,
to clear the channel the length of my childhood.

# FAINT ASTRONOMY

The stars are dairy candy, but we grow up
to congregate in their light like children with
torn pockets. Someone is always a rookie,
in a profusion of blossoms someone is always
heavier than usual, tired and unastounded.
Must someone's ripening always be miserable?
Must the cashier, between downpours, tell us
it's weather lovely "for ducks," although the duck
in his natural canvas has not been shortchanged.
Is wild growth the inevitable bane of what we call
"our lives?" The farmer, corncrop quartered by rains,
is pointing his finger at the manager of the reservoir.
Soon the rasp of the katydid, chirp of the cricket
and the first red plume in the sumac will overcome
the summer sun's instructions. It must have been winter
when Stevens called the sun "brave." Winter surely
is the family's family-time, and then the stars':
bones of the dark, thin beams on which
our wishes ride their colossal specificities
right into Heaven, winking to let us know.
Yet the star dies. The sea praises and withdraws.
If we could dwell for a moment solely on the ugly,
for that moment we would not think evil
an imbalance in the universe, and for a while yet
it might be possible to linger in good company,
looking up to the even-handed star-display
for something to cut up six ways from Sunday.
But these stars are beautiful, and do not bully the
                                                    sublime.
They give us waste-time, while we try to find the planets.

# IOWA LAND

O barn reality! I saw you swimming
clear across the cornfields of Iowa,
the loveliness and loneliness of you
deeper than the shadows of photographs.

It is a human desire! To lie down
in the damp fall on that black soil
is a human desire. To want to leave
the nuisance of the bed: its small deaths.

It can't just be done. We are born into
a life of avoidance, to the sun
and the tiny seeds of grains,
to the growth of the children.

A man who wakes early works in a field.
Time's what he knows of the end of time.
And he has something to do and what's
to die from—who's close to many, closer to one.

# WHAT'S NEXT?

Somewhere in this Art, there must be Life.
Very serious, and very beautiful, and yet
Who would have thought so even yesterday?

"I think my heart is broken," she says,
And that is Art. "I think I'll never love
Again," says he, and that, too, is Art.

Meanwhile, Life, everywhere opposed
And so dependent on Art, absolutely
Regrets and refuses and goes on kicking.

Not just kicking, but High-kicking!,
The unbroken Heart foreshortens in a smile,
Which seems to say, "That much? —Then show me!"

## & SON

*Of course* no one knows what I'm up to,
But that is fair. The illustrations themselves
Cannot satisfy every reader, though it helps
To have been a good sport, and in any case the notion

Is now outdated that we are to have a good time.
Coming late to a popular movie, I thought
I wouldn't stand in that long a line to see
The end of the world, though immediately it occurred

To me we were all standing in just such a line,
Sometimes seeming to clamor for the show to begin.
This is one of life's qualities, and of course
I accept it: that one is where one doesn't want to be.

For quality and service, however, any store advertising
General Merchandise having in its sign the words
"& Son" will prove dependable wherever located.
If earnings are high, the lamps will burn all night.

# THE HURT TREES

I

These are bit black flowers
on a scruffy winter plane:
a pure mid-country poetry.

Heaven has come down to earth
like rain to dry crackers,
in fact as sleet to these branches,

like: chance, functioning with elegance.
The dead leaf and the globe
and our elastic yearnings

wind in the mind around limbs
which we call "fingers,"
or "heaven," that goal for cows.

II

And we put life into stones.
Without us, stones have already
the still lives of stones,

but we are not satisfied.
To float a stone,
to obtain the key,

the sense of the stars taking
their positions, the fullness
of the earth come round,

one day away
from the duplicate repertoires,
we would have given our lives.

III

For a line inside, for
one line from inside,
we furnish these passages, these

honeycombed catacombs so far from light
the stars offer their past,
these mind-corridors with their

worst that is not over,
and their own stones, and own winters,
their strung trees.

IV

And there was a highway!
A large stone on the road
meant something around the curve.

Your death left you for a moment.
A heavy foot kicked you from behind.
Do you speak English, eh?—

because what you see will be foreign
to you, and foreign to nature,
but made by nature nonetheless:

a man in pain,
a woman in pain,
an accident of nature.


v

And it is wholly an accident
that you were ever there to see it
in that country you summered in,

long before,
before the winter that hurt the trees
and made your eyes water.

## MARVIN BELL

Marvin Bell was born August 3, 1937 in New York City, and grew up in Center Moriches, on the south shore of Long Island. He has lived in upstate New York, Chicago, Indianapolis, Santa Cruz and San Francisco, Vermont, Mexico and Iowa City—where he teaches for The University of Iowa. His poems have won the Lamont Award of The Academy of American Poets, the Bess Hokin Award from POETRY Magazine, and an Emily Clark Balch Prize from THE VIRGINIA QUARTERLY REVIEW.